Teach Your Child

100

WORDS

TO READ, WRITE, SPELL & DRAW

An Animal Coloring Book

Written & Illustrated By Anna Miriam Brown

The Thinking Tree Publishing Company LLC 2016
Copyright 2016 Do Not Copy - WWW.DysLexiaGames.com

MASTER 100 COMMON WORDS

That Every Child Should Know

How to Read and Spell by Age 10

All	Fur	Play	Swim
And	Good	Playing	Take
Are	Grass	Please	Tall
Be	Green	Pond	Teeth
Black	Grey	Raccoon	That
Blue	Have	Race	The
Can	Help	Red	Through
Clouds	Hide	Run	Tiger
Coat	High	Say	To
Could	House	Sea	Treat
Dark	How	See	Trees
Day	In	Shark	Under
Do	Jump	Sharp	Very
Eat	Jumping	Sitting	Warm
Eight	Just	Sky	What
End	Kangaroo	Sleep	When
Fast	Like	Snack	White
Find	Little	Snow	Wild
Fly	Look	So	Win
Flying	Looks	Soft	Wish
Free	Mine	Splash	With
Free	Not	Squirrel	Would
Friends	On	Such	You
From	Place	Summer	Your
Fun	Plate	Sun	Zebra

FUN ANIMAL
WORD GAMES

To Help Your Child Learn How

To Read, Write, Spell and Draw!

INSTRUCTIONS
FOR PARENTS OR TEACHERS:

1. Read each poem four times, pointing to each word as you read it. Many of the words are sight words that do not follow the rules of phonics. The child must be able to recognize each word visually.

2. Ask the child to repeat after you for the 3rd and 4th readings, the goal is for the child to memorize the rhyme.

3. Provide the child with colorful gel pens and one black gel pen.

4. Help the child to understand the instructions on each page. Sometimes the child will color a spelling word, write a missing word, color a picture or draw the missing part of an animal. Sometimes the child will draw the animal's food and habitat.

GREY SQUIRREL

Grey Squirrel, grey squirrel
I look and I see,
How you jump
from tree to tree.

Grey squirrel, grey squirrel
I would like to be,
Jumping and playing
with you in the trees.

COLOR ME!

GREY SQUIRREL

Grey squirrel, grey squirrel
I **LOOK** and I **SEE**
How **YOU** jump
FROM tree **TO** tree

Grey squirrel, grey **SQUIRREL**
I would **LIKE** to **BE,**
Jumping **AND** playing
with **YOU** in **THE** trees.

Note to Parents or Teachers:
Read each poem one more time and ask the child
Point at, say, and color the special words with gel pens.

Draw my Food & Habitat:

GREY SQUIRREL

Grey squirrel, grey squirrel

I **look** and I **see**

How **you** jump

from tree **to** tree

Grey squirrel, grey <u>squirrel</u>

<u>I</u> would **like** to **be**,

Jumping **and** playing

with **you** in **the** trees.

GREY SQUIRREL

Grey Squirrel, grey squirrel

I LOOK and I see

How you jump

from tree to tree

Grey Squirrel, grey squirrel

I would LIKE to be,

Jumping and playing

with you in the trees.

ZEBRA

Zebra, zebra
I look and I see
How you run
so wild and free.

Zebra, Zebra
I would like to be,
Running and jumping
so wild and free.

COLOR ME!

ZEBRA

Zebra, ZEBRA
I LOOK and I SEE
How YOU run
so wild AND free.

Zebra, Zebra
I would LIKE to BE,
Running AND jumping
SO wild AND free.

Draw my Food & Habitat:

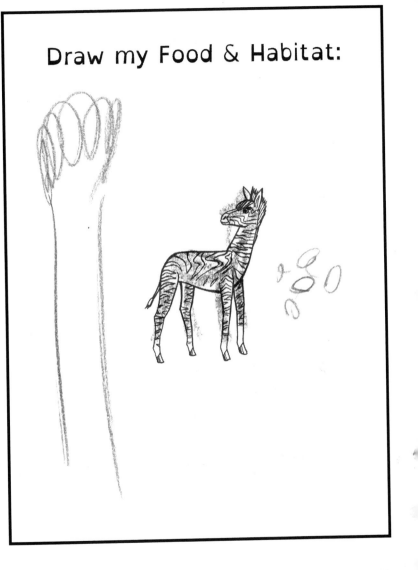

ZEBRA

Zebra, Zebra
I look and I see
How you run
so wild and free.

Zebra, Zebra
I would like to be,
Running and jumping
so wild and free.

Draw the Missing Part:

PLATYPUS

Platypus, platypus
I look and I see
How you swim
so wild and free.

Platypus, Platypus
I would like to be,
Swimming and Splashing
so wild and free.

COLOR ME!

PLATYPUS

Platypus, platypus
I LOOK AND I see
HOW you SWIM
so WILD and FREE.

Platypus, Platypus
I WOULD like to BE,
Swimming AND Splashing
so WILD and FREE.

Draw my Food & Habitat:

PLATYPUS

Platypus, platypus

I look and I see

How you swim

so wild and free.

Platypus, Platypus

I would like to be,

Swimming and Splashing

so wild and free.

Draw the Missing Part:

KANGAROO

Kangaroo, kangaroo
What do you eat?
Are grass and leaves
Your favorite treat?

Kangaroo, Kangaroo
What do you do?
I would like to jump
with you.

COLOR ME!

KANGAROO

Kangaroo, KANGAROO
WHAT do you EAT?
ARE GRASS AND leaves
YOUR favorite TREAT?

Kangaroo, Kangaroo
WHAT do you DO?
I WOULD like to JUMP
WITH you.

Draw my Food & Habitat:

KANGAROO

Kangaroo, KANGAROO
What do you Eat?
Are grass and leaves
Your favorite Tree?

Kangaroo, Kangaroo
What do you Do?
I would like to jump
With you.

Draw the Missing Part:

RACCOON

Raccoon, raccoon

What do you eat?

Look in a trashcan

for your favorite treat.

Raccoon, Raccoon

What did you find,

when you dumped

that trashcan

COLOR ME!

RACCOON

Raccoon, RACCOON
WHAT do YOU EAT?
LOOK in A trashcan
for YOUR favorite TREAT.

Raccoon, Raccoon
WHAT did YOU FIND,
WHEN you dumped
THAT trashcan

Draw my Food & Habitat:

RACCOON

Raccoon, _____

____ do ___ ___?

____ in _ trashcan

for ____ favorite _____.

Raccoon, Raccoon

____ did ___ ____,

____ you dumped

____ trashcan

Draw the Missing Part:

BLUE JAY

Blue jay, blue jay
What do you eat?
Is your favorite snack
worms and seeds?

Blue jay, Blue jay
Do you like to fly
with the clouds
high In the sky?

COLOR ME!

BLUE JAY

BLUE jay, blue jay
WHAT do YOU eat?
Is YOUR favorite SNACK
worms AND seeds?

Blue jay, Blue jay
DO you LIKE to FLY
WITH the CLOUDS
HIGH in the SKY?

Draw my Food & Habitat:

BLUE JAY

＿＿＿＿ jay, blue jay

＿＿＿＿ do ＿＿＿ eat?

Is ＿＿＿＿ favorite ＿＿＿＿＿

worms ＿＿＿ seeds?

Blue jay, Blue jay

＿＿ you ＿＿＿＿ to ＿＿＿

＿＿＿＿ the ＿＿＿＿＿＿

＿＿＿＿ in the ＿＿＿?

Draw the Missing Part:

LION CUB

Lion cub, lion cub

Are you having fun?

You play all day,

In the warm summer sun.

Lion cub, lion cub

Pounce and run!

Playing all day,

looks like such fun!

COLOR ME!

LION CUB

Lion cub, lion cub
ARE you having FUN?
You PLAY all DAY,
In the WARM SUMMER SUN.

Lion cub, lion cub
Pounce and RUN!
Playing ALL day,
LOOKS like SUCH fun!

Draw my Food & Habitat:

LION CUB

Lion cub, lion cub

___ you having ___?

You ____ all ___,

In the ____ _____ ___.

Lion cub, lion cub

Pounce and ___!

Playing ___ day,

_____ like ____ fun!

Draw the Missing Part:

HIPPO

Hippo, hippo

Splash, splash, splash,

In the pond,

you take a bath.

Hippo, Hippo

It looks like fun,

swimming and splashing

in the sun!

COLOR ME!

HIPPO

Hippo, hippo
Splash, SPLASH, splash,
In the POND,
you TAKE a bath.

Hippo, Hippo
It LOOKS like FUN,
swimming AND splashing
IN the SUN!

Draw my Food & Habitat:

HIPPO

Hippo, hippo

Splash, _____, splash,

In the ____,

you ____ a bath.

Hippo, Hippo

It _____ like ___,

swimming ___ splashing

__ the ___!

Draw the Missing Part:

GIRAFFE

Giraffe, giraffe
Tall as can be!
You are as tall
as the leafy trees!

Giraffe, Giraffe
Do you like to eat,
Yummy green leaves,
From very tall trees?

COLOR ME!

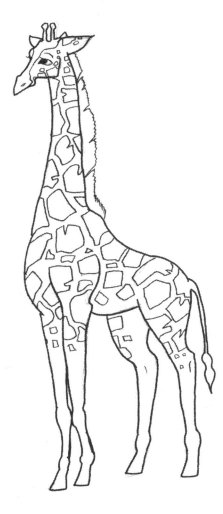

GIRAFFE

Giraffe, giraffe
TALL as CAN be!
You ARE as TALL
as THE leafy TREES!

Giraffe, Giraffe
Do you LIKE to EAT,
Yummy GREEN leaves,
From VERY tall TREES?

Draw my Food & Habit.

GIRAFFE

Giraffe, giraffe

____ as ___ be!

You ___ as ____

as ___ leafy _____!

Giraffe, Giraffe

Do you ____ to ___,

Yummy _____ leaves,

From ____ tall _____?

Draw the Missing Part:

SMALL MOUTH BASS

Bass, bass,

Do you like to swim,

In the pond,

With your friends?

Please be careful!

Do not take the bate!

You might end up

on someone's plate!

COLOR ME!

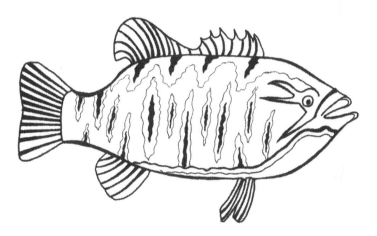

SMALL MOUTH BASS

Bass, bass,
DO you LIKE to SWIM,
In THE pond,
WITH your FRIENDS?

PLEASE be careful!
Do NOT to TAKE the bate!
You might END up
ON someone's PLATE!

Draw my Food & Habitat:

SMALL MOUTH BASS

Bass, bass,

__ you ____ to _____,

In ___ pond,

_____ your _____?

_____ be careful!

Do ___ to ____ the bate!

You might ___ up

__ someone's _____!

Draw the Missing Part:

BLACK JAGUAR

Black jaguar, black jaguar

You have beautiful marks,

You blend with shadows,

In the dark.

Black jaguar, Black jaguar

I wish I could be,

that good at playing,

hide and seek.

COLOR ME!

BLACK JAGUAR

Black jaguar, BLACK jaguar
You HAVE beautiful marks,
YOU blend WITH shadows,
IN the DARK.

Black jaguar, BLACK jaguar
I WISH I COULD be,
that GOOD at playing,
hide AND seek.

Draw my Food & Habitat:

BLACK JAGUAR

Black jaguar, _____ jaguar

You _____ beautiful marks,

_____ blend _____ shadows,

_____ the _____.

Black jaguar, _____ jaguar

I _____ I _____ be,

that _____ at playing,

hide _____ seek.

Draw the Missing Part:

GREAT WHITE SHARK

White shark, white shark

You are so sleek,

in the ocean,

Dark and deep.

White shark, white shark,

you swim so fast,

through the sea,

seeking a snack.

COLOR ME!

GREAT WHITE SHARK

WHITE shark, WHITE shark
You ARE so sleek,
in THE ocean,
Dark AND deep.

White SHARK, white shark,
you SWIM so FAST,
THROUGH the sea,
seeking a SNACK.

Draw my Food & Habitat:

GREAT WHITE SHARK

_____ shark, _____ shark
You ___ so sleek,
in ___ ocean,
Dark ___ deep.

White _____, white shark,
you ____ so ____,
_____ the sea,
seeking a _____.

Draw the Missing Part:

OCTOPUS

Octopus, octopus
You have eight legs.
They help you swim,
and help you play.

Octopus, Octopus
I wish I could be,
Just like you,
Exploring the sea!

COLOR ME!

OCTOPUS

Octopus, octopus
YOU have EIGHT legs.
They HELP you SWIM,
and HELP you PLAY.

Octopus, Octopus
I WISH I could BE,
Just LIKE you,
Exploring THE sea!

Draw my Food & Habitat:

OCTOPUS

Octopus, octopus

___ have _____ legs.

They ____ you ____,

and ____ you ____.

Octopus, Octopus

I ____ I could __,

Just ____ you,

Exploring ___ sea!

Draw the Missing Part:

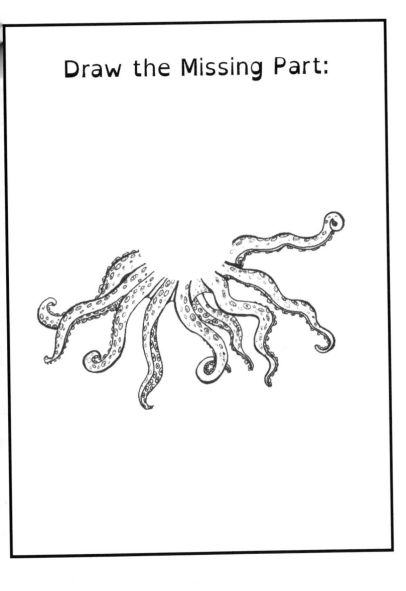

LEMUR,

Lemur, Lemur
Do you like to play?
Do you climb tall trees
every day?

Lemur, Lemur
I wish I could be,
Climbing with you,
In the trees.

COLOR ME!

LEMUR,

Lemur, Lemur
DO you LIKE to PLAY?
Do YOU climb TALL TREES
every DAY?

Lemur, Lemur
I WISH I could BE,
Climbing WITH you,
IN the TREES.

Draw my Food & Habitat:

LEMUR

Lemur, Lemur

__ you ____ to ____?

Do ___ climb ____ _____

every ___?

Lemur, Lemur

I ____ I could __,

Climbing ____ you,

__ the _____.

Draw the Missing Part:

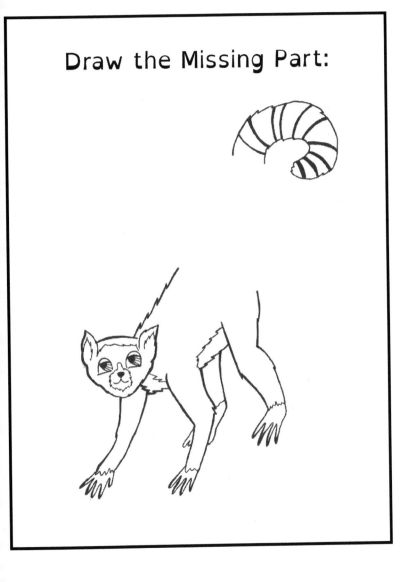

RHINO

Rhino, Rhino

Strong and grey,

sitting in the

sun all day.

Rhino, Rhino

I suppose,

You have a horn,

upon your nose!

COLOR ME!

RHINO

Rhino, Rhino
Strong AND grey,
SITTING in the
SUN ALL DAY.

Rhino, Rhino
I suppose,
You HAVE a horn,
upon YOUR nose!

Draw my Food & Habitat:

RHINO

Rhino, Rhino

Strong ___ grey,

_____ in the

___ ___ ___.

Rhino, Rhino

_ suppose,

You ____ a horn,

upon ____ nose!

Draw the Missing Part:

RED FOX

Red fox, red fox
Do you like to sneak
through the snow
on mountain peaks?

Red fox, red fox,
Run and hide.
You sleep all day
and play all night.

COLOR ME!

RED FOX

RED fox, red fox
DO YOU LIKE to sneak
through THE SNOW
ON mountain peaks?

Red fox, RED fox,
RUN AND HIDE.
You SLEEP ALL day
AND PLAY ALL night.

Draw my Food & Habitat:

RED FOX

___ fox, red fox

__ ___ ____ to sneak

through ___ ____

__ mountain peaks?

Red fox, ___ fox,

___ ___ ____.

You _____ ___ day

___ ____ ___ night.

Draw the Missing Part:

BEAVER

Beaver, beaver,

Cut down a tree,

And build a house

With your sharp teeth!

Beaver, beaver

I wish I could

build as well as you

with wood.

COLOR ME!

BEAVER

Beaver, beaver,
Cut down A TREE,
And build A HOUSE
WITH YOUR SHARP TEETH!

Beaver, beaver
I WISH I could
build as well AS YOU
WITH wood.

Draw my Food & Habitat:

BEAVER

Beaver, beaver,

Cut down ⸏ ⸏⸏⸏⸏,

And build ⸏ ⸏⸏⸏⸏⸏

⸏⸏⸏⸏ ⸏⸏⸏⸏ ⸏⸏⸏⸏⸏ ⸏⸏⸏⸏⸏!

Beaver, beaver

⸏ ⸏⸏⸏⸏ I could

build as well ⸏⸏ ⸏⸏⸏

⸏⸏⸏⸏ wood.

Draw the Missing Part:

TIGER

Tiger, tiger,

Do you like to play,

with your friends,

every day?

Tiger, tiger,

You can run so fast.

Your soft fur coat,

is orange and black.

COLOR ME!

TIGER

Tiger, TIGER,
DO YOU LIKE TO PLAY,
WITH YOUR friends,
every day?

Tiger, tiger,
YOU CAN RUN SO FAST.
YOUR SOFT FUR COAT,
is orange AND BLACK.

Draw my Food & Habitat:

TIGER

Tiger, ⸏⸏⸏⸏⸏,

⸏⸏ ⸏⸏⸏ ⸏⸏⸏⸏ ⸏⸏ ⸏⸏⸏⸏,

⸏⸏⸏⸏ ⸏⸏⸏⸏ friends,

every ⸏⸏⸏?

Tiger, tiger,

⸏⸏⸏ ⸏⸏⸏ ⸏⸏⸏ ⸏⸏ ⸏⸏⸏⸏.

⸏⸏⸏⸏ ⸏⸏⸏⸏ ⸏⸏⸏ ⸏⸏⸏⸏,

is orange ⸏⸏⸏ ⸏⸏⸏⸏⸏.

Draw the Missing Part:

ELEPHANT

Elephant, elephant
Large and grey,
In the safari,
you like to stay.

Elephant, Elephant
You like to play.
If you could talk
what would you say?

ELEPHANT

Elephant, elephant
Large AND GREY,
IN THE safari,
YOU LIKE TO stay.

Elephant, Elephant
YOU LIKE TO PLAY.
IF YOU could talk
WHAT WOULD YOU SAY?

Draw my Food & Habitat:

ELEPHANT

Elephant, elephant

Large ___ _____,

__ ___ safari,

___ _____ __ stay.

Elephant, Elephant

___ _____ __ _____.

__ ___ could talk

_____ _____ ___ ___?

Draw my Food & Habitat:

DRACO LIZARD

Draco, draco

Tiny little thing!

Not just a lizard,

a lizard with wings!

Draco, draco

Black and green,

flying and jumping,

from tree to tree!

COLOR ME!

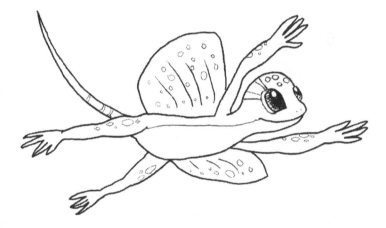

DRACO LIZARD

Draco, draco
Tiny LITTLE thing!
NOT JUST A lizard,
a lizard WITH wings!

Draco, draco
BLACK AND GREEN,
FLYING AND JUMPING,
FROM TREE TO TREE!

Draw my Food & Habitat:

DRACO LIZARD

Draco, draco
Tiny _____ thing!
___ ____ _ lizard,
a lizard ____ wings!

Draco, draco

_____ ___ _____,

_____ ___ _____

____ ____ __ ____!

Draw the Missing Part:

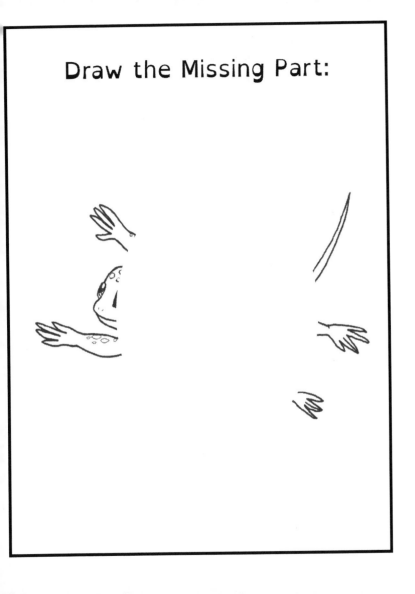

CHEETAH

Cheetah, cheetah,

Win the race!

Swiftly run,

from place to place!

Cheetah, Cheetah

Wild and free!

Dash and run and

play with me!

COLOR ME!

CHEETAH

Cheetah, cheetah,
WIN THE RACE!
Swiftly RUN,
FROM PLACE TO PLACE!

Cheetah, Cheetah
WILD AND FREE!
Dash and run and
PLAY WITH ME!

Draw my Food & Habitat:

CHEETAH

Cheetah, cheetah,

___ ___ ____!

Swiftly ,

▫▫▫▫ ▫▫▫▫▫ ▫▫ ▫▫▫▫▫!

Cheetah, Cheetah

▫▫▫▫ ▫▫▫ ▫▫▫▫!

Dash and run and

▫▫▫▫ ▫▫▫▫ ▫▫!

Draw the Missing Part:

SEA TURTLE

Sea turtle, sea turtle,

Under the sea.

Swimming and playing,

down in the deep.

Sea turtle, sea turtle,

Under the sea.

Swimming and playing

wild and free!

COLOR ME!

SEA TURTLE

Sea turtle, sea turtle,
Under THE sea.
Swimming AND PLAYING,
down IN THE deep.

Sea turtle, sea turtle,
UNDER THE SEA.
Swimming AND PLAYING
WILD AND FREE!

Draw my Food & Habitat:

SEA TURTLE

Sea turtle, sea turtle,

Under ___ sea.

Swimming ___ _____,

down __ ___ deep.

Sea turtle, sea turtle,

_____ ___ ___.

Swimming ___ _____

____ ___ ____!

Draw the Missing Part:

Fun-Schooling

PRACTICE
TIME
Read, Write & Spell

WRITE A SPELLING WORD IN EACH BOX:

ALL
AND
ARE
BE
BLACK
BLUE
CAN
CLOUD
COAT
COULD
DARK

WRITE A SPELLING WORD IN EACH BOX:

DAY
DO
EAT
EIGHT
END
FAST
FIND
FLY
FLYING
FREE
FRIEND
FROM

WRITE A SPELLING WORD IN EACH BOX:

FUN
FUR
GOOD
GRASS
GREEN
GREY
HAVE
HELP
HIDE
HIGH
HOUSE
HOW

WRITE A SPELLING WORD IN EACH BOX:

IN
JUMP
JUMPING
JUST
LIKE
LITTLE
LOOK
LOOKING
LOOKS
MINE
NOT
ON

WRITE A SPELLING WORD IN EACH BOX:

PLACE

PLATE

PLAY

PLAYING

PLEASE

POND

RACCOON

RACE

RED

RUN

SAY

SEA

WRITE A SPELLING WORD IN EACH BOX:

SEE
SHARK
SHARP
SITTING
SKY
SLEEP
SNACK
SNOW
SO
SOFT
SPLASH
SQUIRREL

WRITE A SPELLING WORD IN EACH BOX:

SUCH
SUMMER
SUN
SWIM
TAKE
TALL
TEETH
THAT
THE
THROUGH
TIGER
TO
TREAT
TREES

WRITE A SPELLING WORD IN EACH BOX:

UNDER
VERY
WARM
WHAT
WHEN
WHITE
WILD
WIN
WISH
WITH
WOULD
YOU
YOUR
ZEBRA

WRITE A SPELLING WORD IN EACH BOX:

All

And

Are

Be

Black

Blue

Can

Cloud

Coat

Could

Dark

WRITE A SPELLING WORD IN EACH BOX:

Day

Do

Eat

Eight

End

Fast

Find

Fly

Flying

Free

Friends

From

WRITE A SPELLING WORD IN EACH BOX:

Fun

Fur

Good

Grass

Green

Grey

Have

Help

Hide

High

House

How

WRITE A SPELLING WORD IN EACH BOX:

In

Jump

Jumping

Just

Kangaroo

Like

Little

Look

Looks

Mine

Not

On

WRITE A SPELLING WORD IN EACH BOX:

Place

Plate

Play

Playing

Please

Pond

Raccoon

Race

Red

Run

Say

Sea

WRITE A SPELLING WORD IN EACH BOX:

See

Shark

Sharp

Sitting

Sky

Sleep

Snack

Snow

So

Soft

Splash

Squirrel

WRITE A SPELLING WORD IN EACH BOX:

Such

Summer

Sun

Swim

Take

Tall

Teeth

That

The

Through

Tiger

To

Treat

Trees

WRITE A SPELLING WORD IN EACH BOX:

Under

Very

Warm

What

When

White

Wild

Win

Wish

With

Would

You

Your

Zebra

USE THESE WORDS TO WRITE A STORY OR POEM

All

And

Are

Be

Black

Blue

Can

Cloud

Coat

Could

Dark

USE THESE WORDS TO WRITE A STORY OR POEM

Day

Do

Eat

Eight

End

Fast

Find

Fly

Flying

Free

Friends

From

USE THESE WORDS TO WRITE A STORY OR POEM

Fun

Fur

Good

Grass

Green

Grey

Have

Help

Hide

High

House

How

USE THESE WORDS TO WRITE A STORY OR POEM

In

Jump

Jumping

Just

Kangaroo

Like

Little

Look

Looks

Mine

Not

On

USE THESE WORDS TO WRITE A STORY OR POEM

Place

Plate

Play

Playing

Please

Pond

Raccoon

Race

Red

Run

Say

Sea

USE THESE WORDS TO WRITE A STORY OR POEM

See

Shark

Sharp

Sitting

Sky

Sleep

Snack

Snow

So

Soft

Splash

Squirrel

USE THESE WORDS TO WRITE A STORY OR POEM

Such

Summer

Sun

Swim

Take

Tall

Teeth

That

The

Through

Tiger

To

Treat

Trees

USE THESE WORDS TO WRITE A STORY OR POEM

Under

Very

Warm

What

When

White

Wild

Win

Wish

With

Would

You

Your

Zebra

Fun-Schooling
CREATIVE
WRITING
Draw, Write & Spell

WRITE A STORY ABOUT YOUR PICTURE:

DRAW AN ANIMAL

WRITE A STORY ABOUT YOUR PICTURE:

DRAW AN ANIMAL

WRITE A STORY ABOUT YOUR PICTURE:

DRAW AN ANIMAL.

WRITE A STORY ABOUT YOUR PICTURE:

DRAW AN ANIMAL

WRITE A STORY ABOUT YOUR PICTURE:

DRAW AN ANIMAL

WRITE A STORY ABOUT YOUR PICTURE:

DRAW AN ANIMAL

WRITE A STORY ABOUT YOUR PICTURE:

DRAW AN ANIMAL

WRITE A STORY ABOUT YOUR PICTURE:

DRAW AN ANIMAL

WRITE A STORY ABOUT YOUR PICTURE:

DRAW AN ANIMAL

WRITE A STORY ABOUT YOUR PICTURE:

DRAW AN ANIMAL

WRITE A STORY ABOUT YOUR PICTURE:

DRAW AN ANIMAL

Made in the USA
Middletown, DE
20 July 2016